The

MW00910046

Retaining Talent

by

Joanne G. Sujansky, Ph.D.

The Keys to Motivating & Retaining Talent

Copyright (c) 2003 by KEYGroup. All Rights Reserved.

KEYGroup

1800 Sainte Claire Plaza
1121 Boyce Road
Pittsburgh, PA 15241
Business (724) 942–7900 ● Fax (724) 942–4648
www.joannesujansky.com

The material presented in this book is intended for informational use only and should not be construed as legal, accounting or business advice.

ISBN: 0–9654465–3–0

Cartoons by Derek Reed
Cover design by Droz and Associates

Contents

Why People Leave

There are many reasons good employees leave. Some are searching for more balance in their work and personal lives. Others are searching for more challenging, meaningful work. Some want more training opportunities and experiences on the job that allow them to grow and to be more marketable. Others want more money, better benefits. Some say they leave because they don't feel appreciated or connected to their bosses. Others say leadership was lacking in the organization. Any one of these reasons or a combination of a few can cause someone to leave. This book focuses on keeping the talent that you want and need to keep.

KEEP THE "KEEPERS"

#1

Priority:
RETENTION

Make retention a top priority. Focus on it. Talk about it. Never lose talent just because you neglected to pay attention to what's important.

Recruit good talent, tell them what you want, let them know what they did right, have a game plan, encourage them, correct them, celebrate with them, feel the pain with them, push them hard, know their limits.

Decide whom you want to retain. You may not want to retain everyone, nor retain everyone in the same way. Decide how positions contribute to your business and design a retention strategy around this assessment.

10

Gather information at exit interviews about why people leave and share that information with those who need to hear the reasons so they can do something about it.

Get creative about your benefit plan. Employees may have more sophisticated needs in this area than you thought possible. For example, some companies now offer shopping services, adoption reimbursements and even pet care and pet insurance for employees.

Thursday   Friday

14

Seriously consider flexible work schedules. This could include longer workdays and shorter workweeks. Be creative about building in the flexibility.

Stay attuned to employees' needs for life balance. Employees are sensitive to keeping work life, home life and community life in balance. They may stay up all night to finish a special project, but over the long term they won't sacrifice family and friends for the sake of their jobs.

Provide development and learning opportunities. These include formal training, as well as mentoring. Employees want to be marketable.

Provide challenging and meaningful work. Employees do not want to be bored, and they want to know how their work fits into the company's big picture.

Shape and share your vision. Your team members want to know where the organization is going. They also want that to be translated into direction for them. They want you to lead.

LEAD THE WAY

Help team members to "see it in their heads." When they have a clear picture of what can be, it helps them to focus and hopefully motivates them to act. It fosters positive, creative and synergistic thinking.

"Go to bat" for your staff. When they see you fight for resources for them and policies that would help them, they feel more valued.

Partner with your team members. Working collaboratively toward desired outcomes bonds them together so that they solve problems and seize opportunities better and faster.

Show team members that you are committed to the organization. Speak highly of the company and its future whenever you can. Team members want to be proud of their workplace.

Delegate tasks to others that you enjoy doing. Others may well enjoy them, too. They may learn something new or may feel privileged to have been given the work.

Develop a dynamic performance management process. Be sure that specific goals are set for each staff member, that coaching occurs regularly, that periodic reviews against objectives are conducted and that the annual review includes a discussion of a development plan.

Fix what's broken, whether it's a machine or a process. People don't need to be burdened by problems that could be corrected.

40

Don't micromanage.
Employees expect freedom
combined with frequent,
honest feedback.

FIND DIVERSE TALENT

Terminate people who are not contributing. Don't ignore poor performers, as they are sure to hurt the morale of the high performers.

Build a diverse team.
Different perspectives,
experiences, education
and ages enrich the
environment.

Re-recruit your existing talent. It's an opportunity to match their current skills to existing positions within the organization. It's also an opportunity to discuss development possibilities and potential future assignments.

Acknowledge the uniqueness and nurture the different strengths of each of your team members. Different things are important to them and they are each motivated by different things.

Vanilla **?**

52

Address diversity, especially multicultural/generational differences. Customize your coaching techniques to the uniqueness of each team member. Acknowledging differences respectfully can make people feel valued.

Surround yourself with competent people. Skilled, talented employees want to work with others like themselves.

WANTED!
Disputes
Disagreements
Challenges
call:
1-800-DIS-PUTE

Invite different opinions. Don't be defensive. Team members may have valid reasons for their concern about a decision you are making or a plan you've put into action. Hear them out!

COACH THE "PLAYERS"

Do it right now!

Coach and facilitate more.
The "I tell/you do" method of
management simply does not
work for retaining people.

Allow mistakes of yourself and others. When people know that mistakes are understood as a part of the experience, they'll be more creative and take more risks.

Correct constructively. Offer information on ways for your staff to improve and to attain or surpass desired results. Most people are grateful for the suggestions and the attention to their progress.

Give praise freely, but consider the receiver. Although praise seems to be a motivator for everyone, some prefer to receive their praise privately, others like it publicly . . . the grander the better.

Recognize and celebrate even small accomplishments frequently. Employees appreciate spontaneous, positive recognition along the way instead of a delayed recognition during a performance review.

Relay praise. If you've heard someone praise one of your team members, let that person know of the praise. Add some of your own.

Give varied and frequent rewards employees can enjoy. Some appreciate theatre or sporting event tickets, others an afternoon off from work.

Encourage team members to coach each other. The encouragement, teaching and support increases dramatically when all team members provide it.

MAKE WORK
A BETTER PLACE

Bring joy back into the workplace. When people enjoy their work, when the climate is positive, when people laugh and smile often, resilience and productivity are higher.

80

Involve people early in any changes you are considering that may affect them. They will very likely enhance the process and they will feel more committed to the changes and to the organization.

Frequently connect with your team members. Encourage them. Show interest in their work. Challenge them. The climate will become more motivating for them and for you.

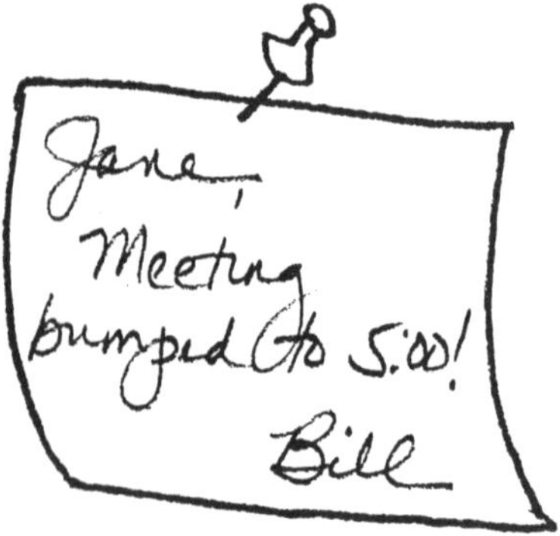
Jane,
Meeting
bumped to 5:00!
Bill

Keep employees informed. If you do not convey current information, the grapevine does, and grapevine information might be distorted.

Say thank you. It can be done in a moment in the hallway. It might be done by a phone call or drop-in visit. It can be written or spoken or both. It's a powerful phrase . . . it can make a person really feel appreciated.

Listen "between the lines." People will show you what they are feeling by their actions and reactions. Pay attention to what concerns them and what "turns them on."

Show that you care. When you show that you care about them and treat them as your most valuable resource, they will reciprocate . . . they'll care back.

Write personal notes of congratulations, condolence, encouragement, get well and thank you. Your staff and colleagues will appreciate it and you will stand out as a leader with heart.

Stay in touch with previous employees. You might be provided an opportunity to bring them back or they may identify other talent for you to recruit.

Give team members a reason to trust you. Tell them the truth, follow through on your promises, keep confidences. They are less inclined to leave when they are in a trusting environment.

Joanne G. Sujansky, Ph.D., CSP

For more than twenty-five years Joanne Genova Sujansky, Ph.D, CSP (Certified Speaking Professional) has been helping leaders increase productivity and inspire loyalty. Her experience, insight, wisdom, humor and practical solutions have made Joanne a highly sought-after speaker for keynote addresses, seminars, conferences, and workshops. She has helped executives and audiences in over 30 countries around the globe, with topics such as:

- Three Keys to Leadership
- Making Change Happen
- Motivating & Retaining Talent

Joanne is an award-winning entrepreneur who, earlier in her career, held management and director level positions across several different industries. She is past National President of the American Society for Training and Development (ASTD), and the recipient of their highest honor, the Gordon M. Bliss Award. Joanne is active in the National Speakers Association, holding their highest earned designation, Certified Speaking Professional.

Copies of **The Keys to Motivating & Retaining Talent**
and other titles may be purchased by contacting:

KEYGroup
1800 Sainte Claire Plaza ● 1121 Boyce Road
Pittsburgh, PA 15241
724–942–7900 (Bus) ● 724–942–4648 (Fax)
www.joannesujansky.com
email: sales@joannesujansky.com

- ❑ The Keys to Conquering Change:
  100 Tales of Success. $19.95
- ❑ The Keys to Motivating & Retaining
  Talent. $6.95
- ❑ The Keys to Mastering Leadership:
  101 Practical Tips. $6.95
- ❑ The Keys to Putting Change in Your Pocket:
  Making Change Work For You. $6.95

The Keys to Conquering Change:
- ❑ Video (VHS) $39.95
- ❑ Video CD $59.95
- ❑ Audio CD $14.95

*Ask about quantity discounts for organizations,
counselors, educators, trainers and speakers.*

Derek P. Reed

Derek Reed is a 16-year old student at Hopewell High School in Pennsylvania. He is an artist who also enjoys photography, skiing, tennis, team handball, golf and travel.

Derek also illustrated *Training Games for Managing Change: 50 Activities for Trainers and Consultants, The Keys to Conquering Change: 100 Tales of Success,* and *The Keys to Leadership: 101 Practical Tips.*

He is currently exploring careers in the field of illustration and advertising. Wherever he goes his employer is sure to value not only his art talent but also his delightful sense of humor.